Original title:
Crystals in the Dark

Copyright © 2024 Swan Charm
All rights reserved.

Author: Paula Raudsepp
ISBN HARDBACK: 978-9916-79-657-3
ISBN PAPERBACK: 978-9916-79-658-0
ISBN EBOOK: 978-9916-79-659-7

Etchings of Light in the Obsidian

In the dark where whispers sigh,
Stars begin to dance and fly.
Ghostly trails of silver thread,
Mapping stories of the dead.

Veils of shadows softly part,
Revealing dreams that warm the heart.
Time entwined with dusk's embrace,
Etchings drawn on night's dark face.

Glow of the Enigmatic Night

Moonlight drapes the world in grace,
Secrets linger, time must trace.
Every corner breathes a tale,
In this twilight, whispers sail.

Neon hues from dreams collide,
Cloaked in mist where shadows hide.
Together, form a mystic dance,
Inviting all to take a chance.

Dusk's Shimmering Array

The sun dips low, a fiery crown,
Colors burst without a frown.
Twilight paints the sky so bold,
A canvas rich, a sight to hold.

Crickets chirp their evening song,
Echoes sweet where hearts belong.
Each moment glows, a fleeting spark,
In this dance from light to dark.

Ethereal Glints in Silent Places

Beneath the hush of sleeping trees,
Where time flows softly with the breeze.
Glints of magic, lightly sown,
In hidden realms, where dreams are grown.

Night unfolds its velvet cloak,
Nature breathes and softly spoke.
In these quiet, sacred grounds,
Whispers echo, timeless sounds.

Celestial Whispers Beneath the Night

Stars whisper dreams, soft and bright,
Moonlight dances, a gentle sight.
Winds carry secrets, old and wise,
As shadows weave through velvet skies.

A quiet hush blankets the earth,
In this darkness, find your worth.
The universe holds each hidden spark,
Guiding souls through the dark.

Silver beams trace the river's bend,
While night's embrace begins to blend.
Echoes of laughter, faint and clear,
In the stillness, they draw near.

Constellations map our dreams' flight,
Charting paths through endless night.
With each flicker, hope takes wing,
Awakening the joy we bring.

In the heart of night's sweet embrace,
We find our voice, our sacred space.
Celestial whispers guide our way,
As the stars reveal a brand new day.

Shimmering Memories of the Unseen

In the twilight where shadows play,
Memories shimmer, drifting away.
Echoes of laughter, whispers of youth,
Paint the past with strokes of truth.

Each moment captured in soft refrain,
A dance of joy, a touch of pain.
Fleeting glances of days gone by,
Like fireflies flickering in the sky.

Time's river flows, carrying dreams,
Through the fabric of memory's seams.
Fragments of laughter, glimpses of grace,
Etched in the heart, a timeless place.

The unseen threads weave stories untold,
In the silent corners, memories unfold.
A mural painted in shades of the past,
Reminding us echoes forever last.

With every heartbeat, memories call,
Shimmering softly, we rise and fall.
A tapestry woven with love's embrace,
In the quiet moments, we find our place.

So gather the stardust, cherish the light,
Embrace the whispers of day and night.
For shimmering memories help us see,
The beauty of life, eternally free.

Shimmering Heartbeats in the Void

In shadows deep, the echoes dare,
A pulse that dances in the air.
Stars twinkle bright, a cosmic play,
As silence whispers, night turns to day.

Each heartbeat swallowed by the night,
A melody lost to the starlit flight.
Fleeting moments, forever spun,
In the vastness, we are one.

Twilight's Palette of Hidden Shine

Brushes dipped in shades of dusk,
Painting dreams in twilight's husk.
The horizon blends in soft embrace,
Where colors merge, time finds its place.

Whispers of lavender, hues of gold,
Stories of night in silence told.
In every stroke, a spirit weaves,
A tapestry of what believes.

Veils of Enchantment in the Night

A veil of mist, soft and light,
Hides the magic of the night.
Stars canine sing their ancient tale,
While shadows weave a glittering veil.

Moonlight dances on the ground,
In this realm where dreams are found.
The heartbeat of the world slows near,
As enchantment whispers, ever clear.

Soft Glows in the Quiet Hour

In the stillness, soft glows rise,
Flickering lights in velvet skies.
Crickets serenade the lonely night,
Cradling moments in gentle light.

Time drifts slowly, a tender sigh,
As dreams take wing, they learn to fly.
In the quiet, hearts gently soar,
Soft glows lingering, forevermore.

Shadows of Radiance Unraveled

In twilight's grasp they softly sway,
Flickers of light that fade away.
Whispers of dusk in a lingering haze,
Reveal the night's elusive maze.

Like silhouettes on canvas bright,
Dancing softly in the night.
Threads of silver, woven tight,
Unravel dreams, take flight in flight.

Celestial Glimmers in the Unknowing

Stars ignite the velvet skies,
Secrets held where silence lies.
Wonders bloom in shadowed nights,
Glimmers chase the fading lights.

Questions linger in the dark,
Each twinkle holds a future spark.
Beyond the veil of what we see,
Lies the realm of mystery.

Beacons in the Midnight Mist

Fog cloaks paths where wanderers tread,
Yet, lanterns shine where dreams are fed.
A soft glow in the settled gloom,
Guides the heart, dispels the doom.

Through the murky, hint of grace,
Light breaks through the woven space.
Each step forward, fears dismissed,
Hope emerges from the mist.

Unheard Echoes of Luminescent Dreams

In silence, echoes softly hum,
Songs of futures yet to come.
Distant visions weave and gleam,
Carving paths through night's bright seam.

Floating whispers touch the soul,
Illuminated, they make us whole.
Through darkened halls, with courage paired,
Our luminous dreams are boldly declared.

Fragments of Radiance in the Abyss

In shadows deep, where whispers play,
Fragments of light dance and sway.
Each glimmer holds a silent tale,
Of dreams once bright, now faint and pale.

Through veils of night, hope flickers near,
Guiding hearts that dare to steer.
In the abyss, stars softly gleam,
A promise held within a dream.

Lost echoes drift on currents low,
In depths where hidden wonders grow.
Victory found in the faintest spark,
Illuminating paths through the dark.

Along these trails, courage ignites,
Lighting the way on endless nights.
Though dangers linger in the deep,
Fragments of radiance help us leap.

With open minds and fearless hearts,
We gather strength from these lost parts.
Together we'll weave a tapestry bright,
Of fragments glowing in the night.

Secrets Encased in Midnight's Hold

Veils of night drape worlds untold,
Secrets encased in shadows bold.
Whispers echo through silent trees,
Carried soft on the night breeze.

In the stillness, mysteries bloom,
Enigmas wrapped in twilight's gloom.
Each star a key to unlocking fate,
Revealing paths that patiently wait.

Hidden dreams beneath the stars,
Guarded closely, despite their scars.
In the heart of darkness, courage reigns,
Unraveling threads of forgotten chains.

Shimmering truths bathe in the moon,
As shadows hum a calming tune.
Secrets shared with the dawn's first light,
Transforming fears into pure delight.

Through midnight's grasp, we journey forth,
Chasing the hopes that give us worth.
Encased in trust, we find our way,
To illuminate the break of day.

The Lure of Illuminated Depths

Beneath the waves where silence sings,
The lure of depths, a treasure brings.
Coral gardens, colors bright,
Whisper secrets, lost to night.

In azure realms, time ebbs and flows,
Where sunlight dances, and magic grows.
Beneath the surface, wonders lie,
Calling forth the curious eye.

Deep in the ocean's warm embrace,
Secrets bloom in this hidden place.
With every pulse, adventure calls,
Through shadowed depths where starlight falls.

Ancient stories carved in stone,
The heart of mystery is never alone.
In swirling currents, we find our grace,
The lure of depths, a safe space.

So dive within this mystic deep,
Where dreams are sewn and silence keeps.
Illuminated by the moon's soft glow,
The ocean's secrets gently flow.

Bedtime Stories of Glinting Stones

As twilight falls, the stars appear,
Bedtime tales we hold so dear.
Glinting stones that softly shine,
Share their secrets, old and fine.

Each pebble whispers tales of yore,
Of ancient paths and distant shores.
Under blankets, imagination flies,
Carried forth on silver skies.

Moonlit glimmers craft the night,
In stories woven with pure delight.
Fables of courage, dreams anew,
Are spun from gems in softest hue.

Close your eyes and drift away,
To lands where glinting stones will play.
In every heart, a story grows,
A tapestry of cosmic prose.

So let the night cradle your dreams,
With shimmering stones and silver beams.
Bedtime stories, sweet and bright,
Guide you gently through the night.

Illumination Behind Closed Eyes

In the still of night, thoughts align,
Dreams awaken, softly they shine.
Whispers of hope float in the air,
Guiding the heart, banishing despair.

Bright visions dance in the mind's embrace,
Each fleeting moment, a tender grace.
Stars and secrets twinkle within,
The journey begins where shadows thin.

With every breath, a story unfolds,
Mysteries whispered, quietly told.
A canvas of thoughts bathed in light,
Illumination breaks the night.

Behind closed eyes, we find our way,
Through valleys of dreams where shadows play.
The world outside fades into the past,
In this realm of peace, we're free at last.

Glimmering Veils of Nightfall

As dusk descends, a curtain drawn,
Glimmers of gold meet the coming dawn.
Veils of silence cover the ground,
In whispers of twilight, lost dreams are found.

Stars peek out from a velvet sky,
Gaze wrapped in wonder as time drifts by.
The moon hangs low, casting a spell,
In glimmering hues, all is well.

Gentle breezes weave tales anew,
Threads of fate in the fading blue.
Magic lingers where shadows blend,
An elegant dance that has no end.

Crickets serenade the tranquil night,
Soft harmonies bask in silver light.
Each moment precious, like fleeting breath,
In glimmering veils, life conquers death.

Glistening Mosaic of Secrets

Fragments of life in colors bright,
A mosaic woven, hidden from sight.
Pieces of laughter, sorrow, and grace,
In the heart's gallery, a sacred space.

Whispers of stories blend into one,
Glistening paths where shadows run.
Every shard tells a tale profound,
In silence, the secrets are forever found.

Memories shimmer like stars in the dark,
Each glimmer a whisper, a longing spark.
A tapestry lived, with threads intertwined,
In the clutches of time, our truths align.

The journey unfolds, a delicate weave,
In every moment, new dreams conceive.
A glistening mosaic of all we hold dear,
As the heart embraces all that is near.

The Silence of Sparkling Shadows

In the hush of night, shadows softly sigh,
Sparkling like secrets, they linger nearby.
Echoes of memories whisper low,
In the silence of twilight, our feelings flow.

Each flicker of light tells a story untold,
Of dreams that were chased and thoughts that were bold.
Moments preserved in the quiet abyss,
Where shadows dance gently, a fleeting bliss.

Stillness surrounds, a comforting veil,
In the space between heartbeats, we sail.
Through sparkling shadows, we wander free,
In the silence, we find who we'll be.

Time drifts like whispers on the breeze,
In the calm of the night, our worries ease.
Together we dream, as the world fades away,
In the silence of shadows, forever we stay.

Hidden Light Beneath the Veil

In shadows deep, a whisper sighs,
A flicker glows, where silence lies.
Beneath the dark, a secret waits,
A hidden spark that radiates.

Through woven mist, the light will break,
A gentle pulse, a tender ache.
With every tear, it softly gleams,
A guardian of forgotten dreams.

It dances slow, like autumn leaves,
In twilight's hush, it gently weaves.
A tapestry of hope displayed,
In quiet hearts, its joy is laid.

From veils of night, it finds its way,
To guide the lost, to light their day.
With every glance, it casts a glow,
A warmth to cherish and to grow.

So seek the light in darkest times,
In every shadow, truth still shines.
For hidden bright beneath the veil,
Lingers hope, a whispered trail.

Twinkling Secrets in the Gloom

In the silence of the night,
Stars reveal their secrets bright.
Whispers dance on a cool breeze,
Carried softly through the trees.

Glimmers peek through heavy clouds,
Shy and soft, like hidden crowds.
Each twinkle tells a tale of old,
In every flicker, stories unfold.

The moon adds silver to the scene,
Casting shadows on the green.
In the gloom, the magic swells,
Twinkling secrets, nature tells.

Among the dark, they wait and play,
Guiding dreamers on their way.
In the vastness of the night,
Twinkling secrets shine so bright.

Hold these moments close and dear,
Each star a wish that draws us near.
In the tapestry of the sky,
We find the dreams that never die.

Dancers Among the Starlit Dusk

In the quiet of the night,
Dancers twirl in soft twilight.
With every step, they spin and sway,
Embracing darkness, welcoming day.

Underneath a velvet sky,
They leap and laugh, their spirits fly.
Each movement filled with grace and light,
A celebration of the night.

Moonbeams cast a silver glow,
Illuminating dreams we know.
Silent rhythms guide their pace,
In this magical, sacred space.

As stars glow bright, they weave and spin,
A dance of joy, where love begins.
Wrapped in the warmth of sweet delight,
With every twirl, they shine so bright.

In the dusk, they find their chance,
To hold the world in a fleeting glance.
With laughter ringing through the trees,
They celebrate the night's soft breeze.

Reflections on an Obsidian Tide

On obsidian waves, the night unfolds,
A mirror to secrets, deep and bold.
The sea whispers of untold dreams,
As shadows dance with silver beams.

In the tide's embrace, we find our place,
A depth of thoughts, a tranquil space.
The moonlight paints the water's skin,
A shimmering path where thoughts begin.

Each ripple tells a story of old,
Echoing secrets that time has told.
As the tide ebbs, reflections glow,
Unveiling truths that start to flow.

We stand in wonder, hearts aligned,
In the dark waters, we are refined.
With every wave that breaks and sighs,
We glimpse the light that never dies.

So let the obsidian tide embrace,
The dreams we chase, the fears we face.
In every glance, we find the art,
Of reflections caught within the heart.

Iridescent Murmurs of the Night's Heart

In the stillness of the night,
Whispers float like fleeting dreams,
Stars blink soft, a gentle sight,
Moonlight dances, silver beams.

Petals fall, each with a tale,
Breath of secrets in the air,
Night's embrace, a velvet veil,
Shadows linger without care.

Softest sighs upon the breeze,
Nature speaks a silent truth,
Rustling leaves, the world at ease,
Echoes weave the threads of youth.

In the dark, the heart does shine,
Pulse of life in rhythmic beat,
Ancient songs that intertwine,
Capture moments bittersweet.

Whispers blend with dreams of old,
In the silence, stories bloom,
Iridescent, softly told,
Night's heart beats without a gloom.

Whispers of Ancients Beneath Dim Light

Beneath the glow of ancient flame,
Echoes stir from shadows cast,
Voices murmur, know their name,
Stories live, and time flows fast.

Crickets sing in harmony,
Moonlit paths reveal their lore,
Guided by the melody,
Ancients linger evermore.

Roots entwined with destinies,
Wisdom shared through rustling leaves,
Hidden deep, the mysteries,
Nature's hymn that never grieves.

Underneath the starry skies,
Ghosts of dreamers walk the night,
With each breeze, a soft reprise,
Ancient whispers take their flight.

Lost in time, yet ever near,
Legends thrive in twilight's veil,
Listen close and you will hear,
The heart of night begins to sail.

Shimmering Tides of Ancestral Memories

Waves roll in with tales untold,
Salt and sand, the past remains,
Histories in colors bold,
Ebb and flow with whispered gains.

Every tide brings forth a dream,
Fleeting shadows on the shore,
Underneath the silver gleam,
Memories dance, a timeless roar.

Seagulls cry, like voices lost,
Carried far by ocean's breath,
Each wave counts the heavy cost,
Of those who drifted into death.

Yet in the depths, a light still shines,
Ancestral tales beneath the waves,
Their spirits sing in rhythmic lines,
Guiding us through the darkest caves.

As the sun dips, colors blend,
Shimmering paths of ages gone,
In each wave, a message send,
Embracing dusk till break of dawn.

Chasing Ghosts of Radiant Echoes

In twilight's grasp, we seek the past,
Shadows dance in fleeting light,
Chasing ghosts that fade so fast,
Echoes whisper through the night.

Softly glows a distant star,
Promises that linger near,
In the dark, we wander far,
Voices calling, faint yet clear.

Hearts beat like the falling rain,
Pulses race with every glance,
Haunted by a sweet refrain,
Lost in time, we join the dance.

Every laugh, a memory spun,
Every sigh, a fleeting chance,
In the shadows, we are one,
Chasing ghosts in a timeless trance.

With every step on this worn ground,
Radiant echoes guide our way,
In the silence, love is found,
Whispered secrets softly stay.

Echoes of Dusk's Elegance

Whispers of twilight softly glide,
As shadows stretch and dreams abide.
In hues of pink and deepening blue,
Stars awaken, a chosen few.

Reflections dance on the silver lake,
Each wave a secret, each ripple a wake.
Nature holds its breath in awe,
As day surrenders to evening's law.

Crickets sing sweet serenades,
In the embrace of twilight's shades.
Moonlight spills on the velvet ground,
While the world holds still, profound.

Softly now, the night unfolds,
With stories whispered and untold.
In this canvas of fading light,
Beauty breathes, kissed by night.

Echoes linger, softly fade,
In the moment dusk has made.
An elegy for the sun's descent,
Embraced by the night, content.

Silhouettes of Hidden Radiance

Among the shadows, secrets hide,
In every nook, a whisper wide.
Figures of lore in the pale moonlight,
Dance in silence, taking flight.

Gentle breezes carry tales,
Of forgotten dreams in forgotten trails.
Each silhouette, a mystery born,
In the soft hush of the early morn.

Underneath the stars' watchful eyes,
Hope flows freely, never dies.
Radiance cloaked in the dark,
Hints of the day, a flickering spark.

The night reveals what day concealed,
In shadows woven, hearts revealed.
Each breath, a promise of things to come,
In silence spoken, they softly hum.

Fading into the dawn's embrace,
Echoes fade without a trace.
Yet the essence of what was there,
Lives on in whispers, sweet and rare.

Veiled Luminescence

In the stillness, a glow appears,
Shrouded in mystery, calming fears.
Veils of night drape over the sky,
Sparking wonders that draw the eye.

Soft light dances on leaf and stone,
Illuminating paths where dreams have grown.
Glimmers flicker, a gentle tease,
In the embrace of the evening breeze.

Crimson hues blend with sapphire night,
Creating a canvas that feels just right.
Colors merge, a symphony bold,
Stories of wonder waiting to be told.

Each flicker a promise of bright tomorrows,
Transforming shadows, easing sorrows.
Veiled luminescence, so sweet and bright,
Guides the lost through the velvet night.

From veils unfurled where hopes take flight,
Shimmers of possibility ignite.
In the quiet, magic does reside,
Awakening dreams that softly glide.

Shimmering Depths of Night

In the depths where shadows sleep,
Mysteries in silence creep.
Stars like jewels, scattered light,
Guide the wanderers through the night.

Moonlit waters, calm and clear,
Reflecting whispers we long to hear.
Ripples hold the night's embrace,
Stories woven in time and space.

The air is chill, yet hearts are warm,
In the night's embrace, we feel transformed.
Gentle dreams drift on the air,
Bathed in starlight, beyond compare.

Every echo a promise made,
In shimmering depths, we won't be swayed.
Journey on, for the night is young,
While songs of old are softly sung.

Embrace the stillness, the beauty near,
In the quietude, we lose our fear.
Shimmering depths of a velvet sky,
Hold the secrets we long to fly.

Moonlit Echoes of Prismatic Thoughts

In the silence of the night,
Whispers dance with pale moonlight.
Colors blend in soft embrace,
Creating dreams in silent space.

Shadows flicker, thoughts take flight,
Chasing echoes 'til the light.
Reflections paint the skies so bright,
In the realms where stars ignite.

Glistening beams of silver sheen,
Travel paths where we have been.
In the stillness, truths unwind,
As the universe aligns our minds.

Waves of light, they ebb and flow,
Eternal secrets we both know.
With every pulse, the world expands,
In the warmth of gentle hands.

Beneath the gaze of twilight's grace,
Hidden wonders softly trace.
Moments caught in breathless sighs,
Moonlit echoes never die.

The Veiled Light Within

In the depths of quiet dreams,
Lies a light that softly gleams.
Wrapped in layers, safe and sound,
A secret place where truths are found.

With each heartbeat, shadows fade,
Illuminated paths displayed.
A gentle flame that flickers near,
Reveals the heart's most cherished fear.

As night whispers its sweet refrain,
The veiled light brings calm from pain.
In solitude, the spirit soars,
Unlocking all the hidden doors.

Every sigh, a tale untold,
In this sanctuary, brave and bold.
Radiant sparks in silent night,
Burst into life with pure delight.

So let the stillness guide your way,
Let the inner light hold sway.
For in the dark, you'll find the spark,
Of the veiled light that warms the dark.

Shining Treasures of the Night

Stars like diamonds in the sky,
Whisper secrets, oh so high.
Each a story, old yet new,
Glimmering in the velvet hue.

Moonbeams dance on waves of blue,
Carrying dreams, both fresh and true.
In the stillness, memories spark,
Lighting paths that wander dark.

Winds of whispers softly tease,
Through the branches of the trees.
Ancient echoes softly call,
In twilight's grace, we rise, we fall.

Close your eyes and feel the glow,
Treasures found in ebb and flow.
In the night, our hearts unite,
Embracing all the shining light.

For every shadow hides a gem,
Each night's an unseen diadem.
In the depths of dark, we see,
The shining treasures meant to be.

A Symphony of Glimmers in Stillness

In the hush where silence sings,
Stars compose on silver strings.
Notes of light in gentle sway,
Guide our souls along the way.

Every spark, a soft refrain,
Echoes through the quiet gain.
In each twinkle, stories flow,
As the heartbeats gently glow.

In twilight's arms, we find a place,
Time unwinds its soft embrace.
Moments glisten, moments pause,
In the rhythm, silence draws.

A symphony of calm so bright,
Whispered dreams in cloaks of night.
Let the stars their music weave,
In stillness, we begin to believe.

Cradled in the arms of fate,
We discover what awaits.
In the glimmers, hearts entwined,
A symphony of souls aligned.

Glimmers of the Night

Stars twinkle softly in the dark,
Whispers of dreams begin to spark.
Moonlight dances on the ground,
In the silence, solace is found.

Gentle breezes sing their song,
Lifting shadows all along.
Night wraps the world in its embrace,
A velvet cloak, a sacred space.

Glistening dewdrops line the grass,
Moments fleeting, too quick to pass.
Each glimmer holds a tale untold,
In the night, such magic unfolds.

Step into realms of mystery,
Where whispers weave a tapestry.
Echoes of time, a tender grace,
In twilight's arms, a warm embrace.

Glimmers fade as dawn draws near,
Yet memories linger, crystal clear.
Hold the magic, let it shine bright,
Within your heart, keep the night.

Shards of Shadow's Embrace

In shadows deep, where silence lies,
The heart of night softly sighs.
Fragments dance in a muted glow,
Hiding stories that we do not know.

Whispers cling to the chilly air,
Specters linger, yet none beware.
Each shard reflects a time long past,
Echoes of dreams that fade so fast.

Beneath the moon's soft, silver hue,
The world transforms, a place anew.
Embrace the shadows, let them guide,
In secret places, where secrets bide.

Light and dark in a tender blend,
A dance of forces that never end.
In the quiet, find your trace,
Within the shards of shadow's embrace.

As dawn approaches, shadows flee,
Yet leave their mark in memory.
Hold the secrets close, let them stay,
In the heart's chambers, night lives on day.

Luminous Whispers at Midnight

Midnight brings a golden glow,
Luminous whispers play below.
Stars align in the vast expanse,
Inviting souls to take a chance.

In this hour, all is still,
Dreams awaken, bend to will.
Voices dance in the starlit haze,
Crafting tales of ancient ways.

Softly beams the moon's embrace,
Cradling night with gentle grace.
Each whisper holds a promise bright,
Guiding hearts through the twilight.

Moments linger, suspended time,
Brushing past in a rhythm sublime.
In the lull, truths reveal,
Midnight's magic, oh, so real.

As dawn's light begins to creep,
Cherish dreams and vows to keep.
In luminous whispers, find your flight,
Through the stillness of the night.

Echoes of Shimmering Silence

Silence dances on the breeze,
Carried softly through the trees.
Echoes shimmer in the air,
Whispers weave a moment rare.

In still reflections, secrets hide,
Within the hush where souls abide.
Gentle glimmers fade to gray,
Yet linger on, to softly sway.

Each heartbeat marks a fleeting hour,
Nature wakes, revealing power.
Silent songs of the world unfold,
Stories waiting to be told.

As shadows stretch and twine,
In the stillness, stars align.
Echoes linger, their notes divine,
In the tapestry of space and time.

Wrap the night around your heart,
Where echoes whisper, never part.
In shimmering silence, find your light,
Guided gently through the night.

Silenced Symphony of Celestial Glow

In the stillness of the night,
Stars whisper tales of old,
A melody lost to the winds,
In silence, their stories told.

Moonlight dances on the ground,
Casting shadows, soft and bright,
Each shimmer a note unplayed,
In the symphony of night.

Echoes drift through the air,
Gentle tunes fade away,
Life in the cosmos carries on,
Though the music may betray.

Golden hues paint the skies,
As dawn begins to break,
The quietude sings sweetly now,
In every breath we take.

We'll remember the quiet songs,
Of the universe's grace,
In the silence, a beauty lies,
In the vastness, a warm embrace.

A Tapestry of Light in Dusk's Embrace

When day gives way to night,
The horizon starts to glow,
Threads of amber and violet,
Weave a wondrous show.

In the skies, colors melt,
Like whispers of the wind,
A canvas painted softly,
Where daylight's song rescinds.

Beneath the stars' soft glow,
Shadows begin to weave,
The tapestry of dusk blooms,
In the night, we believe.

Each twinkle tells a story,
Of dreams yet to unfold,
In this embrace of twilight,
A beauty to behold.

With every fading echo,
Nature's brush sets the tone,
In the hush of dusk's transition,
We find we are not alone.

Glimpses of Magic in the Murk

In the depths where shadows lie,
Whispers of magic gleam,
A flicker, a fleeting glance,
Life flows like a dream.

Through the fog, enchantments call,
Starlit secrets intertwine,
Finding joy amidst the gloom,
In a world so divine.

Murk and mystery converge,
An allure we can't ignore,
Each moment holds a promise,
Of wonders to explore.

Breathe the air, filled with hope,
Trust the path that you find,
In the hidden corners of dusk,
Magic can unbind.

The night wraps us in wonder,
A canvas of twilight hue,
In every glimpse of magic,
Life beckons anew.

Glimmers in the Shadows

In the corners of the night,
Glimmers softly play,
Hidden sparks of brilliance,
Chasing the dusk away.

Beneath the curtains of dark,
Whispers start to form,
The shadows may hold secrets,
Yet life is not forlorn.

Flickers caught in moonlight,
Dance among the leaves,
In this quiet symphony,
The heart of night receives.

Every shadow, every gleam,
Bears a tale untold,
In the stillness, there's a magic,
In the dark, we behold.

Let the glimmers guide us,
Through paths we dare to roam,
In the interplay of shadows,
We find our way back home.

Celestial Glow Beneath the Surface

In the depths where shadows dwell,
A radiant spark begins to swell.
Secrets hide in silent streams,
Whispers of forgotten dreams.

Moonlight dances on the tide,
Flowing gently, like a guide.
Stars are born in velvet night,
Awakening the hidden light.

Beneath the surface, calm and deep,
Ancient stories softly seep.
Roots of light entwined in fate,
Drawing near, we contemplate.

With each wave, a tale unfolds,
Of shimmering threads and secrets told.
A universe of vivid hues,
In the stillness, color brews.

Hold the glow within your grasp,
Feel the warmth, let shadows clasp.
Each glimmer tells its own refrain,
In celestial hopes, we remain.

Whispering Light Beneath Obscurity

A flicker stirs in muted gloom,
Painting bright the darkened room.
Echoes dance upon the wall,
Whispers of the light's soft call.

Through the haze, a shimmer breaks,
Softly flowing like the lakes.
Murmured tones of dusky night,
Carried through the gentle flight.

Behind the veil, the glow persists,
In breaths of air and misted trysts.
Subtle warmth entwines the bare,
All in silence, light lays bare.

Caught between the dark and dawn,
Each flicker's story newly drawn.
Illuminated hope ignites,
In the shadows, truth invites.

Embrace the whispers, soft and low,
For in the dark, true colors show.
Life unfolds like curtains drawn,
Radiant beneath a hush of dawn.

Transient Glimmers in Unlit Corners

In the corners where light refrains,
Fleeting sparks break mundane chains.
Moments linger, then they flee,
Glimmers fading, wild and free.

Faintly glowing, secrets gleam,
Chasing shadows, chasing dreams.
Unlit paths, a soft embrace,
Transience finds its rightful place.

Time drips like dew from dawn,
Mirrored in the life withdrawn.
Every blink, a chance to see,
Fragments of serenity.

In quiet pauses, truth unveils,
Whispers carried on the gales.
Moments brief, yet rich and bright,
Holding fast the fragile light.

Glimpses gathered, fleeting grace,
Dance of shadows, sweet embrace.
From the dusk, we forge our song,
In transient glimmers, we belong.

The Secret Language of Radiance

Words unspoken sense the air,
A glow emerges, soft and rare.
In every beam, a tale ignites,
Whispers shared in shades of light.

Speaking volumes without sound,
In brilliance, truth is found.
Colors blend, converse in hues,
Echoes of the heart's own muse.

Every ray a brushstroke fine,
Painting paths where shadows shine.
Moments echo in the glow,
Mapping feelings we don't show.

Radiant pulses intertwine,
Our stories gleam through every line.
In stillness, sparks of joy expand,
Illuminating what's unplanned.

In the language soft and clear,
All our hopes and dreams appear.
Gathered under light's embrace,
The world's beauty finds its place.

The Allure of Celestial Fragments

Stars whisper secrets in the night,
Each flicker tells tales of ancient flight.
Galaxies swirl in a cosmic dance,
In the darkness, we find our chance.

Nebulas bloom like flowers of light,
Eclipsing shadows, banishing fright.
Comets streak past with fiery grace,
Leaving behind the void's embrace.

Planets waltz in a silken embrace,
Gravity's pull, a languid chase.
The universe hums a timeless song,
Drawing our spirits where we belong.

Through telescopes, dreams come alive,
In every blink, new worlds thrive.
Celestial fragments, secrets we seek,
In the vast expanse, we find what's meek.

Awake in wonder, navigate the skies,
Following stardust with longing eyes.
In every shimmer, symmetry found,
The allure of the cosmos, forever unbound.

Twinkling Echoes of the Unseen

In the hush of night, whispers unfold,
Stories of stars waiting to be told.
Echoes of twilight dance on the breeze,
Filling the heart with gentle pleas.

From shadows deep, a flicker glows,
The unseen path where mystery flows.
Hidden realms wait in silence to speak,
In twinkling echoes, our souls seek.

With every glint, the cosmos sings,
Of lost loves and forgotten things.
Gentle reminders from worlds afar,
Twinkling softly like a falling star.

Underneath the velvet canopy wide,
Exist realms where secrets reside.
In twilight's embrace, we lose our fears,
In the echoes, we find our tears.

Through the darkness, illumination beams,
Lighting the way for our wildest dreams.
Unseen wonders in a cosmic spree,
Twinkling echoes, forever free.

Shadowed Gemstone Reveries

Beneath the surface, colors entwine,
In shadows cast, treasures align.
Gemstones glimmer, secrets concealed,
In their depths, the heart is revealed.

Emerald dreams in twilight glow,
Whispering tales of long ago.
Sapphires shimmer with stories told,
Hidden beneath the surface, bold.

In velvet darkness, opals gleam,
Mirroring the depths of every dream.
Their radiant hues, a soothing balm,
In shadowed reveries, we find calm.

Rubies pulse with the heat of time,
Chasing echoes of a distant rhyme.
Each stone a memory, each flaw a tear,
In gemstone shadows, we wander near.

To hold their beauty is to embrace,
The whispers of time in a silent space.
In every shadow, a light that beams,
Gemstone reveries, woven in dreams.

The Radiance Beneath the Surface

Dive deep into the ocean's heart,
Where mysteries flow and lives impart.
The surface shimmers with golden light,
But below, wonders ignite the night.

Coral gardens bloom in vibrant hues,
Dancing fish weave through the ocean's blues.
In forgotten depths, the stories whisper,
Of sunken ships and hearts that shimmer.

The gentle current carries the past,
In each wave, a memory cast.
Light refracts in a radiant swirl,
Beneath the surface, magic unfurls.

From shadows cast by ancient stone,
Lives a world where silence has grown.
In this embrace, we find our grace,
The radiance shines in a hidden space.

Awake to marvels beneath the waves,
Where life thrives and water braves.
In the depths, true beauty resides,
The radiance beneath, where wonder abides.

Ethereal Glows in the Depths

In shadows deep where secrets lie,
Ethereal glows dance in the sigh.
Whispers echo through the haze,
While time blurs in a timeless gaze.

Flickers of light on water's chest,
Reveal the treasure, a shrouded quest.
Among the depths, the silence glows,
In dreams where calm serenity flows.

Cradled in dark, a world reborn,
As night unveils an unseen morn.
With every pulse, the spirit beams,
In twilight's embrace, we weave our dreams.

Veils of mist in a tender sweep,
Cloaked in the still, the waters keep.
Glistening trails lead the way,
To places where the lost decay.

With every breath, the stars ignite,
Embedding hopes in blackened light.
A journey onward, forever sought,
In depths of night, our souls are caught.

Hope Cradled in Obsidian Hands

In shadows where the light is thin,
Hope glimmers bright, a spark within.
Obsidian hands, fierce yet kind,
Carry dreams that fate designed.

Cradled gently, the fragile flame,
Against the dark, it whispers name.
A promise held, a love profound,
In silence deep, where souls are found.

Through trials long, the heart stays strong,
Each beat like fire, melodious song.
In depths of night, resilience stands,
Fueled by strength of obsidian hands.

With every tear, a gem is formed,
In struggles faced, our spirits warmed.
We rise anew from ashes laid,
For in the dark, our hopes paraded.

So gather dreams, let shadows lend,
The courage found in every bend.
With hands of night, we shape our dance,
In strong embrace, we seize our chance.

The Beauty Beyond the Veil of Night

Beyond the veil where darkness veils,
Lies beauty wrapped in whispered tales.
Stars whisper softly, secrets spun,
In quiet moments, dreams begun.

Moonlit paths invite our gaze,
With silver sheen, they weave their maze.
In every corner, shadows play,
A masterpiece in hues of grey.

Each breath of night, a soothing balm,
Cradles the world in tranquil calm.
Where silence reigns, and hearts take flight,
We find our truth in endless night.

As dawn approaches, colors blend,
To paint anew, our hearts commend.
Yet in the dark, the essence glows,
The beauty held where stillness grows.

So linger long, embrace the night,
For in its arms lay pure delight.
Beyond the veil, the world transforms,
In shadows, light, the heart adorns.

The Secret Life of Forgotten Jewels

In dusty vaults where time stands still,
Forgotten jewels, with stories fill.
Their spark wears thin, yet shines within,
Whispers of ages, lost and thin.

Each gem a tale, each cut a sigh,
Reflecting glories of days gone by.
Lost in corners of time's embrace,
Faded brilliance holds a trace.

An emerald's gaze, a sapphire's dream,
Capture glimpses of life's bright gleam.
In silence kept, their essence flows,
The secret life that still bestows.

When sunlight touches the dusts of gray,
These treasures wake, in splendor play.
A dance of light, a joy revived,
In shadows deep, their truth survived.

So cherish gems, both bright and worn,
For in their hearts, new lives are born.
In every facet, love persists,
The secret life in twilight's mist.

Beneath the Cloak of Night

Stars whisper secrets low,
Moonlight dances on the ground,
Shadows weave a tale so bright,
In silence, magic can be found.

Gentle breeze through branches sways,
Echoes of the night unfold,
Dreams are born in twilight's haze,
In darkness, stories are told.

Night unfolds its velvet shroud,
Protecting soft, elusive dreams,
In the quiet, shadows crowd,
And light unravels at the seams.

Whispers of the earth arise,
Crickets sing their lullabies,
Beneath the cloak, the heart complies,
In the night, the world complies.

A canvas painted deep and vast,
With starlit hues and midnight's brush,
In silence, memories are cast,
Beneath the night, our spirits hush.

Soft Glows of the Unseen

Beneath the surface, glimmers hide,
Subtle hues that softly gleam,
In shadows where the whispers bide,
Lies the heart of every dream.

A flicker in the darkened space,
Unseen paths that gently thread,
With every heartbeat, we embrace,
The glow that lights the way ahead.

In corners where the light won't creep,
Hidden wonders softly wake,
Secrets held in silence deep,
In darkness, light begins to break.

The softly glowing, unseen tide,
Invites us to explore the night,
For every shadow, there's a guide,
In darkness, find the hidden light.

So let us wander through the dark,
Embrace the glow where shadows lie,
In every corner, every spark,
Soft glows of the unseen will fly.

Twilight's Mosaic of Light

Colors blend as day takes flight,
A tapestry of dusk unfurls,
In harmony, both dark and bright,
The sky, a dance of twirling swirls.

The sun dips low, a fiery hue,
Brush strokes of orange, pink, and gold,
Each moment fleeting, fresh and new,
In twilight's arms, the day is told.

Stars begin their timid glow,
Patching spaces in the night,
A mosaic framing nature's show,
As shadows fade, embracing light.

Each fleeting second, grace bestowed,
Unraveled threads of day's embrace,
With whispers soft where starlight flowed,
A masterpiece, a sacred space.

In twilight's calm, we find our breath,
The world adorned in light's delight,
With every dusk, we conquer death,
In twilight's arms, we find our sight.

Hidden Wonders of the Darkened Realm

In the shadows, secrets play,
Veiled in night, they softly speak,
A realm where whispers tend to sway,
And vivid dreams find refuge, meek.

Softly, echoes trace the round,
Shape of hope that waits in gloom,
In silence, joy is often found,
In hidden realms, the heart will bloom.

Through branches thick, the moonlight peeks,
A world alive with rustling leaves,
In every nook, the spirit seeks,
What night reveals when daylight grieves.

The path ahead may twist and bend,
With every step, a tale begins,
In darkened corners, magic sends,
A spark of joy behind our sins.

In shadows played by starlit scenes,
Nature's treasures, we unearth,
In darkness bright with hidden means,
Wonders wait to show their worth.

The Darkness' Hidden Luster

In the depths where silence stirs,
Stars are veiled, but still they shine,
Whispers echo, soft and pure,
Guiding souls in night's design.

Crimson hues in shadow dance,
Memories flicker, light entwined,
Secrets whisper of romance,
In shadows deep, the hearts aligned.

Beneath the cloak of twilight's sigh,
Hope emerges, radiant and vast,
Stars like diamonds in the sky,
In darkness found, our shadows cast.

Yet in stillness, courage grows,
Every heartbeat finds its place,
In the dark, our true self shows,
Hidden strength, a warm embrace.

Embrace the night, let burdens fly,
For in the luster, dreams await,
Hand in hand, we learn to fly,
In darkness bright, we shape our fate.

Beyond the Veil of Shadow

Beyond the veil, where secrets dwell,
Softly spoken, tales untold,
In whispered dreams, we cast our spell,
As night unfolds its cloak of gold.

Figures dance in midnight's glow,
Silhouetted by the moon's embrace,
Echoes linger, faint and slow,
In the stillness, we find our place.

Through the shadows, light will break,
Glimmers of hope in every heart,
With every step, we dare to wake,
Beyond the night, a brand new start.

Fleeting visions, bright and bold,
In the dark, we chart the course,
Unraveling dreams we long to hold,
For love and light are our true source.

Every moment, fleeting, rare,
Unfolds a story, brave and bright,
Beyond the veil, we learn to dare,
In shadow's depth, we find our light.

Faint Glimmers in Somber Stillness

Faint glimmers flicker in the night,
Casting shadows on the wall,
Hope endures, a fragile light,
In somber stillness, we stand tall.

Echoes of laughter, soft and low,
Drift through air like vapor trails,
In the quiet, our spirits grow,
As the heart of night unveils.

Every whisper tells a tale,
Pointing to the paths ahead,
Through the dark, we shall not fail,
In silence, all our fears are shed.

Stars above, a guiding map,
Drawing dreams from deep within,
Wrapped in night's embrace, we tap,
Into the joy where love begins.

Glimmers shine through every tear,
Painting rainbows in the mist,
In sadness, joy will reappear,
In somber stillness, love persists.

Illumined Threads of Whispered Darkness

Illumined threads weave tales unseen,
In whispered darkness, stories flow,
With every breath, in spaces keen,
We find the light in shadows' glow.

Softly we tread on paths unlit,
Guided by a lantern's grace,
In the quiet, courage is lit,
As whispered dreams begin to trace.

Each heart a spark in vast expanse,
Threads of love, so finely spun,
In moments lost, we take our chance,
To dance until the night is done.

Embrace the thread, the dark divine,
Where secrets linger, soft and sweet,
With every touch, our souls align,
In whispered darkness, two hearts meet.

For in the quiet, bound we glide,
Together, united, hearts ablaze,
Illumined threads, they shall abide,
In every night, our love shall blaze.

Illuminated Silhouettes of Mystery

In the dusk where shadows play,
Figures dance in soft array.
Flickers whisper through the night,
Casting shapes in fragile light.

Secrets linger in the dark,
Echoes of a distant spark.
Veiled in time, a story waits,
In the glow that fate creates.

Beneath the stars that softly gleam,
Illusions weave a silver dream.
In each silhouette, we find,
A glimpse of what the heart designed.

The moon a witness to our sighs,
As mystery unfolds and flies.
Silent tales of love and pain,
In the night, we seek the rain.

As dawn approaches, shadows fade,
Yet in our minds, the visions stayed.
Illuminated, we must part,
With silhouettes etched in the heart.

Midnight's Subtle Spark

In the silence, secrets wake,
Midnight stirs with every ache.
A gentle breeze, a whispered tone,
In the dark, we are alone.

Stars ignite a fleeting fire,
Hope against the creeping dire.
With a flick, the night ignites,
Subtle sparks of lost delights.

Time slows down; the world retreats,
In this glow, our heartbeat meets.
Underneath the cosmic shroud,
We find solace, unbowed.

Shadows dance, a fleeting game,
In our hearts, we feel the flame.
From the depths, desires rise,
Amid the darkness, spirit flies.

As the world turns, we remain,
Chasing shadows, free from chains.
In this moment, love's profound,
Midnight's spark is all around.

Enchanted Shards of the Unknown

Through the woods, a path unclear,
Every rustle, every fear.
Twilight breaks on nature's stage,
Whispers turn the next page.

Shards of light in twilight's grip,
Guide our hearts on this wild trip.
Magic lingers in the air,
With each breath, a silent prayer.

Every corner hides a tale,
In the shadows, dreams unveil.
Through the mist, we wander slow,
Finding secrets in the glow.

Echoes of a distant call,
Calling forth, we rise and fall.
Enchanted shards, we must embrace,
In this realm, we find our place.

As the night begins to weave,
In this dance, we learn to believe.
Each step forward, fears dethroned,
In the magic of the unknown.

Dappled Light in the Shadows

Breaking dawn with subtle grace,
Dappled light begins to chase.
Casting hues on forest floors,
Unlocking nature's hidden doors.

Through the leaves, the sunlight weaves,
Telling tales that the heart believes.
Every ray, a brush of gold,
Painting stories yet untold.

Shadows stretch, then softly play,
In the depths where dreams delay.
Whispers from the twilight past,
In this beauty, we hold fast.

Moments flicker, life's refrain,
Dappled light through joy and pain.
In the dance of sun and shade,
We find solace, unafraid.

As the day begins to fade,
In the twilight, dreams are laid.
Dappled light, forever flows,
In our hearts, its magic grows.

Glimmering Hope in the Shade

In shadows deep where silence dwells,
A whisper soft, a tale retells.
Amidst the gloom, a flicker bright,
Hope glimmers softly, returning light.

Each leaf that rustles, secrets share,
A promise woven in the air.
Through tangled paths, our hearts align,
In shrouded moments, stars will shine.

A gentle breeze, the night's embrace,
Life's tender pulse in a hidden space.
We seek the glow in what is lost,
Glimmers of hope, no matter the cost.

In every sigh, a hint of grace,
A spark ignites, no time to waste.
Embrace the dark, but trust the dawn,
For in the shade, our dreams are drawn.

Together we shine, a match divine,
In quiet corners, our hearts entwine.
Let shadows fade, as wonders keep,
A glimmering hope in memories deep.

Veiled Luminescence: A Quiet Journey

Through misty paths and winding roads,
We seek the light, where silence flows.
Soft whispers guide our steps along,
In veils of night, we find our song.

The moon hangs low, a watchful eye,
Illuminating dreams that softly lie.
With every breath, we draw the night,
In hidden realms, our spirits light.

A tapestry of stars unfolds,
Stories of old, in starlight told.
Each moment framed in gentle grace,
A quiet journey, time's embrace.

Beneath the sky, we've come to find,
The sacred space of heart and mind.
With veiled luminescence shining near,
A path of hope, where love is dear.

As shadows dance, we share our dreams,
A luminous bond, or so it seems.
Together, in this quiet space,
We walk with grace, in love's embrace.

The Twilight of Forgotten Treasures

In twilight's glow, the past awakens,
Twinkling lights where silence beckons.
Forgotten tales, in dust enshrined,
Whispers of time, in shadows blind.

Each treasure lost, a memory's plea,
In echoes soft, where we long to be.
Through faded halls, we tread so light,
In twilight's arms, we seek the night.

The heart recalls what once was near,
A tapestry of joy and fear.
With every breath, the stories weave,
In twilight's fold, we dare believe.

A dance of dreams, in hues of gray,
Forgotten treasures find their way.
With open hearts, we start to see,
The twilight's gift of memory.

As night descends, we hold what's true,
The past illuminated, anew.
In every flicker, each glimmer's trace,
The twilight beckons, time and space.

Secrets of Luminous Lingerings

In shadows cast by gentle light,
The secrets dance, both bold and white.
We wander through the hushed refrain,
In luminous lingerings, truth remains.

Each moment pauses, a breath in time,
In glimmers lost, we start to climb.
The world unfolds in whispers rare,
Secrets tucked in the evening air.

With every step, a pathway glows,
Where thoughts are wrapped in silken flow.
In twilight hues, our hearts will soar,
Exploring all the hidden lore.

Each flicker warms the midnight throng,
In luminous lingerings, we belong.
A tender truth, the night reveals,
As hearts entwined embrace their feels.

In silvery dreams, the world in sway,
Secrets held close, afar they sway.
In whispered tones, we find the key,
To secrets bright, that set us free.

Nocturnal Gleams of Forgotten Tales

In midnight's cloak, whispers call,
Echoes of dreams that rise and fall.
Stars in silence unveil their lore,
Memories linger, forevermore.

Beneath the moon's soft, watchful gaze,
Shadows dance in a gentle haze.
Each flicker tells a story long,
In twilight's heart, they hum their song.

The night reveals paths once concealed,
Adventures hidden, now unsealed.
With every glimmer, a tale unfolds,
In the silence, the magic molds.

Silent sentinels stand so still,
Guardians of dreams that time will fill.
As night unfolds, the past runs deep,
In the realm where secrets sleep.

Nocturnal winds, caress my face,
As I wander through time and space.
Each shadow holds a glistening truth,
In forgotten tales of lost youth.

Twinkling Dreams in the Darkness

In shadows thick, where silence reigns,
Twinkling dreams break through the chains.
Stars play hide and seek with night,
Guiding hearts with soft, warm light.

Mysterious visions start to bloom,
Casting away the weight of gloom.
Each whisper is a tender thread,
Weaving hopes where fears once fled.

Under the veil of velvet skies,
The distant echoes softly rise.
A symphony of sighs and dreams,
In the dark, each flicker beams.

Restless spirits chase the dawn,
In the night, they laugh and yawn.
Magic stirs, and shadows sway,
In twilight's dance, they find their way.

In twilight's hush, our hearts align,
With twinkling dreams, forever fine.
As darkness falls, we turn the page,
And write anew, in bright, bold sage.

Glistening Stories Among Shadows

In corners dim, where memories hide,
Glistening stories come to bide.
Flickering lights in the stillness speak,
Of journeys taken, the brave and meek.

Among the shadows, laughter glows,
Each tale a bloom from a past that knows.
Echoes entwined in the midnight air,
Crafting narratives of hope and despair.

Whispers of love, of loss, of grace,
In the glimmering dark, they find their place.
Through tangled dreams, we wander far,
Guided by an unseen star.

With every sigh, a story stirs,
In the quiet, the heart concurs.
Merging the worlds of light and shade,
In each reflection, a journey made.

As dawn approaches, the whispers fade,
Leaving the night for memories laid.
Yet in the heart, they'll ever throng,
Glistening stories eternally strong.

The Enigma of Unrealized Brilliance

Within the mind, a spark resides,
Dreams unspoken, where hope abides.
Shrouded in layers of silent thought,
The enigma waits, by time forgot.

Glorious visions crave the light,
Yet linger lost in endless night.
A treasure chest, with keys unseen,
Holding brilliance, serene, serene.

Each heartbeat thunders, urging bold,
To chase the dreams, no longer cold.
As shadows coalesce into form,
Whispers of grace begin to warm.

The canvas stretched, colors blend,
To paint a story that has no end.
With every brushstroke, echoes swell,
The unknown speaks, it casts a spell.

As dawn approaches, scars retreat,
Unveiling wonders, bittersweet.
The enigma blooms in radiant fire,
Igniting passions, lifting higher.

Flickering Jewels in the Dusk

Stars emerge in the night sky,
Scattering dreams like fireflies.
Whispers of the evening breeze,
Painting tales among the trees.

Moonlight dances on the lake,
Casting shadows, gentle wake.
Each twinkle holds a secret bright,
Flickering jewels, pure delight.

As darkness wraps the world so tight,
Hope still glimmers, soft and light.
A symphony of quiet grace,
In dusk's embrace, we find our place.

Time slows down beneath this dome,
In the night, we find our home.
A canvas of dreams unfolds anew,
In flickering jewels, we find what's true.

The horizon bends, a soft sigh,
As stars wink down and softly fly.
In twilight's hush, a breath we take,
With every flicker, our hearts awake.

The Radiance of Forgotten Echoes

Whispers linger in the air,
Memories tangled in despair.
Time erases, yet they glow,
In shadows cast, their light will flow.

Faded laughter, echoes sweet,
A haunting rhythm, soft and neat.
Golden moments slip away,
But their radiance still will stay.

Sunbeams chase the morning dew,
Reflecting shades of love so true.
Every sigh, a spark ignites,
Forgotten echoes, shining lights.

In the silence, feel the spark,
Illuminate the endless dark.
With every heartbeat, they arise,
Radiant truths in endless skies.

From the past, they gently weave,
Stories lingering, we believe.
In forgotten echoes, time's embrace,
We find our path, our rightful place.

Enigmatic Light in Hushed Spaces

In corners where the shadows blend,
A mystic light begins to send.
Subtle hues that softly gleam,
Whispered wonders, like a dream.

Candle flames that flicker low,
Unveil secrets we long to know.
In the silence, visions dance,
Enigmatic light, a fleeting chance.

Walls adorned with mem'ries spun,
Recollections of laughter won.
Every glimpse, a silent story,
In hushed spaces, finding glory.

Beneath the folds of gentle night,
Hope ignites in soft twilight.
Amidst the stillness, hearts unite,
In the enigmatic, pure delight.

Every shadow holds its grace,
Revealing truth, time can't erase.
In hidden realms, we find our way,
With elusive light, come what may.

Silent Cries of Twinkling Souls

In the night, we search for peace,
Where the quiet never cease.
Stars above, so far away,
Twinkling softly, they convey.

Silent cries of ancient dreams,
Echo through the galaxy's beams.
Each flicker tells a story grand,
Hearts in shadows take a stand.

Wishes whispered in the dark,
With every twinkle, souls embark.
Eternal journeys born anew,
In silent cries, our spirits grew.

Beneath the vast and starry dome,
We find solace, we find home.
With every blink, we hear the call,
Silent cries, uniting all.

So let us roam through evening's grace,
In the darkness, we find our place.
Twinkling souls, a serene goal,
In silent cries, we find our whole.

Twinkling Relics of the Forgotten

In shadows deep, where whispers dwell,
The stars appear, their secrets tell.
A flicker here, a glimmer there,
Remnants of dreams suspended in air.

Ghostly echoes call from the past,
Memories flicker, too bright to last.
Lost tales weave through the silent night,
Each twinkle a spark, each spark a light.

Ancient paths where time has fled,
The stories linger, the words unsaid.
A canvas painted with joy and pain,
Each relic a story, a shimmered chain.

Dancing softly, the light will sway,
Guiding the lost in their own ballet.
For those who seek, their hearts ignited,
In twinkling relics, hope is invited.

So look to the sky, let sorrows cease,
Find solace in stars, and be at peace.
For in the night, the past will blend,
In twinkling relics, all wounds can mend.

Hidden Radiants in the Night

Beneath the cloak of velvet skies,
The night reveals its quiet sighs.
Glimmers of hope, so faint, yet bold,
In hidden corners, secrets unfold.

A moonbeam's kiss on the whispering trees,
A pulse of light in the gentle breeze.
Silver threads through branches weave,
Promising dreams that we dare believe.

Soft footsteps on the path once lost,
In search of treasures that come at a cost.
Heartfelt wishes ride on the air,
Hidden radiants, beyond compare.

The stars invite us to reach out wide,
To gather the light, let hope be our guide.
For in the dark, the brightest shine,
These hidden gems are yours and mine.

So take a breath, let the night enfold,
Embrace the warmth of stories untold.
In shimmering shadows, our spirits soar,
For hidden radiants offer so much more.

The Underworld's Sparkling Tapestry

In depths unknown, where shadows creep,
A tapestry woven from secrets we keep.
Every thread, a whisper, a sigh,
Embroidered tales from those who lie nigh.

Glistening gems in the muted glow,
Casting reflections of struggles below.
Amidst the darkness, a beauty rare,
In every stitch, a story to share.

The underworld hums a haunting tune,
Among the stars and the slumbering moon.
Each sparkle a memory, fierce and bright,
A reminder of battles fought in the night.

With courage, we tread on this woven path,
Embracing both joy and enduring wrath.
For within each knot, there's a chance to mend,
The underworld's gifts can heal and transcend.

So let the tapestry guide your way,
In sparkling threads, hope finds its sway.
For glimmers of light in the darkest spheres,
Are just reflections of triumph over fears.

Nightfall's Dazzling Treasures

As day gives way to the evening's hold,
A symphony of colors, vibrant and bold.
Nightfall whispers with a gentle grace,
Unveiling treasures in a quiet embrace.

Stars like lanterns adorn the sky,
Each one a promise, a soft lullaby.
Dazzling jewels in the vast expanse,
Inviting hearts to join in a dance.

The moon's tender glow paints paths anew,
Guiding the dreams that chase shadows through.
Night creatures stir with their secret calls,
In nightfall's gleam, magic enthralls.

With every twinkle, a wish takes flight,
Dazzling treasures born from the night.
Hold tightly to hope as horizons blend,
For nightfall's wonders never quite end.

So pause for a moment, let stillness be found,
In the treasures of night, let love abound.
In dazzling darkness, we find our way,
With nightfall's embrace, come what may.

Shards of Midnight Light

In shadows deep, the whispers play,
Fragments of light that drift away.
A silver glint in the velvet night,
Holding secrets, holding fright.

Stars awaken with a gentle grace,
Shattering darkness in a soft embrace.
Each flicker tells of what might be,
A dance of hope, wild and free.

Through tangled dreams, the path unfolds,
In this realm where the night beholds.
A breath of twilight, crisp and bright,
Guiding hearts toward morning light.

Echoes linger where shadows weave,
Stories whispered that we believe.
Each shard a memory, each glow a sign,
A puzzle piece of the divine.

So let us wander, hand in hand,
Through brightened spaces, across the land.
For in these shards, we find our way,
Into the dawn of a new day.

Luminous Secrets Beneath the Veil

Beneath the veil where shadows lie,
Secrets breathe, and faint dreams sigh.
With every rustle, the night will swell,
Whispers shared, enchantments dwell.

In hidden glades where silence reigns,
Luminous echoes break the chains.
Softly glowing, the truth ignites,
Guiding souls to wondrous heights.

The world awakens beneath the skin,
Veiled desires, lost within.
With every heartbeat, stories flow,
Of luminous paths we yearn to know.

Threads of silver intertwine,
In secret places, hearts align.
A dance of fate, of joy and pain,
Beneath the veil, the dreams remain.

From darkness rises a hopeful beam,
Casting visions, sparking dreams.
In luminous hues, reveal the light,
Unravel secrets, chase the night.

Whispered Reflections

In quiet pools, reflections sleep,
Whispered tales the waters keep.
Each ripple tells of moments past,
Fleeting shadows that forever last.

A gaze in silence, memory spins,
The dance of life and where it begins.
Ghostly echoes in the twilight glow,
Speaking softly of all we know.

As night descends, the truth appears,
Whispers rising, calming fears.
In mirrored depths, the thoughts cascade,
Revealing paths that dreams have made.

Ephemeral moments, crystal clear,
In whispered tones, we draw near.
Each reflection a lesson framed,
In quiet whispers, we are named.

So lean into the tranquil stream,
Let thoughts wander where they may dream.
For every whisper, a treasure found,
In the silence, love unbound.

Fragments of Starlit Dreams

In the night sky, dreams unfold,
Starlit fragments, stories told.
A canvas vast of wonders bright,
Where hopes awaken, taking flight.

Each glimmer speaks of wishes cast,
Moments fleeting, but ever vast.
With every spark, a journey starts,
Mending seams of broken hearts.

In the cosmic ballet, we sway,
Chasing dreams that guide our way.
Stars are whispers of the divine,
Mapping paths where souls entwine.

Through the night, in shimmering spells,
Fragments dance, and magic dwells.
A symphony of light and shade,
In starlit dreams, we won't fade.

So look above and feel the call,
For in this beauty, we find our all.
Fragments woven in celestial beams,
Illuminate the path of dreams.

Lurking Brilliance of Forgotten Landscapes

In shadows deep where echoes dwell,
Old stories rise, a silent spell.
Each whisper hints of time unspun,
In golden dusk, lost dreams still run.

Forgotten trails and ancient trees,
Beneath the weight of history's breeze.
The colors fade, yet still they gleam,
A haunting place, a fading dream.

The sun slips low, the sky ignites,
With fading hues of starry nights.
The landscapes hold their secrets tight,
In twilight's glow, a gentle light.

Step carefully on this hallowed ground,
Where pieces of the past are found.
Each stone and stream, a tale to share,
In the stillness, we find our prayer.

So linger here, in silence breathe,
With every turn you may perceive.
The lurking brilliance yet remains,
In forgotten lands where memory reigns.

Veil of Brilliant Murmurs

A soft refrain drifts through the air,
In twilight's hush, a gentle care.
Brilliant murmurs dance like fireflies,
Illuminating dreams where silence lies.

Beneath the stars, in velvet skies,
Whispers float like distant sighs.
Each note weaves tales of days gone past,
In the night's embrace, our hearts beat fast.

The moon unveils a silver sheen,
As shadows pirouette, soft and keen.
Together they sing, the night awakes,
And in their harmony, the world shakes.

In secret corners, magic flows,
With every breath, the wonder grows.
Lost in this veil of sounds divine,
We find ourselves as dreams entwine.

Embrace the dusk, let worries cease,
In brilliant murmurs, we find peace.
The night's embrace, a sweet cocoon,
In whispers shared, we dance with moons.

Glistening Whispers at Midnight

When shadows drape the world in night,
Glistening whispers take their flight.
In quietude, secrets unfold,
A tapestry of stories told.

The stars conspire with the sky,
Each flicker, a soft lullaby.
Silvery threads weave through the dark,
Painting the dreams that dare to spark.

Time stands still in the midnight air,
A moment caught, suspended there.
Each glittering spark, a heartbeat's flow,
In the depths of night, wonders grow.

We listen close, to hear the sighs,
Of memories hidden from watchful eyes.
In the glistening quiet, we find the way,
To navigate through night to day.

So close your eyes, let whispers guide,
In glistening moments, secrets bide.
For in the stillness, treasures lie,
Awakening dreams that will not die.

Secrets of the Star-Kissed Abyss

In the depths where silence reigns,
Secrets hide in shadowed veins.
The star-kissed abyss, a realm untold,
Where mysteries of the night unfold.

Each twinkle holds a story dear,
Of journeys vast, both far and near.
In darkness, whispers find their voice,
Inviting us to make our choice.

Subtle echoes of the past,
In this vastness, memories cast.
Each heartbeat kindles, gently glows,
In the abyss where true love grows.

So venture forth, embrace the night,
In the unknown, discover light.
The secrets wait, both brave and bold,
In the star-kissed depths, tales are told.

With eyes wide open, explore within,
In the whispers of the night, begin.
For every secret found in time,
Is but a step toward the sublime.

The Allure of Obscure Brilliance

In shadows deep where whispers weave,
The beauty lies that few believe.
A spark in dark, a fleeting glance,
An invitation to the dance.

Fleeting stars in the twilight's hue,
Flicker softly, lost just for you.
Mysteries held in silence's call,
In darkness, we see it all.

Unearth the gems that softly glow,
In corners where the dreamers go.
The allure of life, both strange and bright,
Illuminates the endless night.

When quiet reigns, the heart can hear,
The song of night, both bold and clear.
A brilliance found in what is missed,
In every shadow, a gentle twist.

So chase the stars that flicker near,
In every breath, let go of fear.
For in the dark, the soul can soar,
To realms unknown, forevermore.

Midnight's Glories Unseen

Beneath the moon's soft silver grace,
Midnight holds a secret place.
Hidden dreams in velvet night,
Awaken visions, pure delight.

The world is wrapped in quiet sleep,
While starlit tales in silence creep.
Each shimmer holds a whispered wish,
Awaiting time, our hearts to swish.

The night enfolds with gentle arms,
A tapestry of mystic charms.
In every shadow, laughter lies,
A cosmic dance beneath the skies.

With every twinkle, hope ignites,
As midnight sings with soft delights.
The glories wait, though dreams may hide,
In every heart, a faithful guide.

So stand beneath that vast expanse,
And let the stars invite you to dance.
For in the glimmers, truth is spun,
Midnight's glories, her embrace begun.

Secrets of Radiance in the Veil

In morning's mist, a secret brews,
Softly whispered in the hues.
Radiance veiled in gentle light,
Unseen wonders take their flight.

The world awakes, yet still it hides,
A sparkling truth the silence bides.
Founded deep in tranquil grace,
A hidden glow we yearn to trace.

Through tangled paths of shadowed dreams,
The beauty glints in subtle beams.
A dance of light, a fleeting spark,
In realms where day meets the dark.

Secrets weave through every sigh,
As time unfolds, we learn to fly.
With every heartbeat, life's embrace,
Reveals the magic in our space.

So linger not in doubt and fear,
For radiance whispers, ever near.
In every moment, let it sail,
Discover secrets in the veil.

The Hidden Symphony of Glimmer

A symphony of softest gleam,
Plays on the edge of waking dream.
Notes of light in gentle flow,
A hidden song we long to know.

Where shadows twist and soft winds sigh,
The glimmer whispers, time to fly.
In each small ray, a story sings,
Of joyful hopes and wondrous things.

The hidden chords of dusk and dawn,
In silence weave a fabric drawn.
With every pulse, the heart's delight,
Creates the day from heart of night.

The echoes play in soft refrain,
Through every joy, through every pain.
A melody that soothes the soul,
In glimmers bright, we find our whole.

Let music sway beneath the stars,
A symphony that heals all scars.
With every sparkle, let it stir,
The hidden symphony of her.

A Tangle of Glows in Twilight

Whispers of dusk softly sway,
Colors blend as light fades away,
Stars begin to flicker and dance,
In the shadows, dreams take a chance.

The horizon blushes, kissed by night,
Crickets sing under fading light,
Branches cradling secret sighs,
While the moon drapes the world in ties.

Glimmering trails in a dusky haze,
Spirits linger in twilight's gaze,
Echoes of laughter float in the air,
A tangle of glows, a moment rare.

As the evening deepens, hearts unwind,
Moments cherished, solace we find,
With each flicker, stories unfold,
In the twilight's arms, we are consoled.

The night prepares its gentle show,
Painting dreams in a velvet glow,
In this sanctuary, let us dwell,
Where a tangle of glows casts its spell.

Winking Gems of the Abyss

In the depths where shadows lie,
Winking gems catch the eye,
Secrets hidden in flowing tides,
As the ocean's heart confides.

Rippling waves in the moon's light,
Dance like stars in the deep of night,
Each sparkle a whisper, soft, sublime,
Remnants of stories lost to time.

Coral castles, bright and bold,
Guard the treasures, tales untold,
In silken waters' embrace we drift,
This serene, mysterious gift.

Echoes of echoes, call from below,
Waves of wonder, currents flow,
The abyss sings in a lullaby clear,
In the depths, no need for fear.

Winking gems in the ocean's veil,
A tapestry woven, wondrous and frail,
In the dark, light finds its way,
Guiding sailors at the end of the day.

Celestial Embers in the Gloom

Under the weight of the starlit night,
Celestial embers flicker bright,
Amid the gloom, they softly glow,
A tapestry of dreams to sow.

Whispers of the cosmos drift near,
Echoed secrets for those who hear,
Each twinkle a promise, old as time,
In the dark, our spirits climb.

Galaxies swirl in a velvet dome,
Guiding the lost, leading them home,
Through realms of wonder, we journey far,
Traced by the light of a distant star.

In silence, the universe spills its grace,
Kisses our souls in endless space,
For in the gloom, the heart can see,
Celestial embers, wild and free.

Let us dance 'neath this cosmic dream,
Embers of magic forever gleam,
In the night's embrace, we find our tune,
Beneath the watchful eye of the moon.

Aurora Beneath the Surface

In silent waters, secrets thrive,
An aurora dances, bold and alive,
Colors ripple, breathtaking and bright,
Beneath the surface, hidden light.

Fish of fire weave through the dark,
Leaving trails like a shimmering spark,
In the depths, their vibrant parade,
A canvas where dreams are made.

Currents swirl with whispered tales,
As echoes of magic on the gales,
A symphony sung in the cool night's breath,
Resonating life, defying death.

Each flash a story, a heartbeat true,
In the water, a world anew,
Where shadows blend with light's embrace,
In a dance of color, a sacred space.

Beneath the surface, the heart can soar,
As auroras rise and colors pour,
In this quiet realm, let us be free,
Finding wonder in the depths of the sea.

The Night's Glistening Lament

Stars shimmer like tears, softly weep,
The moon sighs a glow, secrets to keep.
In shadows they dance, lost hopes ignite,
A symphony plays in the quiet of night.

Whispers of dreams float through the air,
Embracing the silence, a tranquil affair.
Memories linger, like echoes in dark,
Fading away with the dawn's gentle spark.

In the heart of the night, sorrows take flight,
Stars guide the wanderers, casting their light.
Each twinkle a story, each glow a remark,
A testament fierce to the journeys we embark.

Yet still there's a solace in sorrowful song,
For even the morose can help us grow strong.
Through tears of the night, a new dawn will gleam,
A bridge from the shadows to the light of a dream.

So let the lament be a part of our tale,
For through all the darkness, the heart will prevail.
The night's glistening beauty can sometimes feel tough,
But within every heart, there's more than enough.

Darkness Cradles the Bright

In the depths of the night, calm and still,
Darkness enfolds, like a gentle thrill.
Stars peek through veils of shadows so deep,
In silence they promise, secrets to keep.

Moonlight dances softly on treetops so high,
Illuminating paths where the lost ones cry.
Each twinkle a beacon, a guiding delight,
Reminding our hearts that love conquers fright.

Embrace in the dark, where the lost souls convene,
In shadows we find what's rarely seen.
The beauty of silence, the hush that enfolds,
In contrast to brightness, a story unfolds.

As darkness cradles, the flickers ignite,
A balance of worlds, where day meets the night.
With each tender heartbeat and breath drawn with care,
It's here in the silence, we find what we share.

So let us remember the power of shade,
For in every shadow, there's never a fade.
Darkness may cradle but together we'll shine,
A blend of existence, both yours and mine.

Gems Whispers Beneath Murky Veils

Beneath the still surface, treasures await,
Gems whisper softly, tales of fate.
Veils murky and deep, they cradle the lost,
A shimmering promise, no matter the cost.

The depths hold their secrets, hidden from sight,
Glimmers of color, breaking through night.
With patience we listen, as currents flow slow,
Guiding our hearts where the diamonds all glow.

Each drop a reflection of dreams we once bore,
In shimmers and shadows, our spirits explore.
Beneath murky veils lies the beauty so clear,
A chorus of whispers, inviting us near.

Through struggles and secrets, the gems start to gleam,
Forging new paths with each flicker of dream.
What once felt so murky, now sparkles with grace,
Unveiling the truth in this sacred place.

Let us dive deeper where the mysteries lie,
Unearthing the wonders that quietly sigh.
For gems fractured, broken, yet rich in appeal,
Beneath murky veils, their worth becomes real.

Mysteries Wrapped in Silken Shadows

In silken shadows, mysteries wane,
Whispers entwined in a delicate chain.
Veils of the night drape over the land,
Holding the secrets we scarcely understand.

Glimmers of starlight peek through the folds,
Stories untold and the truth it upholds.
In the hush of the moment, a deep breath we take,
To uncover what lies in the silence we make.

With each gentle rustle, anxieties fall,
Wrapped in the comfort, we answer the call.
A dance of the shadows, where fears dissipate,
Inviting the dreams that we silently await.

The mysteries linger in currents of night,
Awakening senses, inviting the light.
Threads woven softly, in twilight's embrace,
Unraveling wonders that time can't erase.

In silken shadows, our stories expand,
Both fragile and fierce, hand in hand we stand.
For wrapped in these layers, our souls will ignite,
In the tapestry woven of dark and of light.

Milton Keynes UK
Ingram Content Group UK Ltd.
UKHW010228111224
452348UK00011B/587